READY, STEADY, PRACTISE!

Laura Griffiths

Grammar & Punctuation
Pupil Book Year 6

Features of this book

- Clear explanations and worked examples for each grammar and punctuation topic from the KS2 National Curriculum.

- Questions split into three sections that become progressively more challenging:

Warm up

Test yourself

Challenge yourself

- 'How did you do?' checks at the end of each topic for self-evaluation.

- Regular progress tests to assess pupils' understanding and recap on their learning.

- Answers to every question in a pull-out section at the centre of the book.

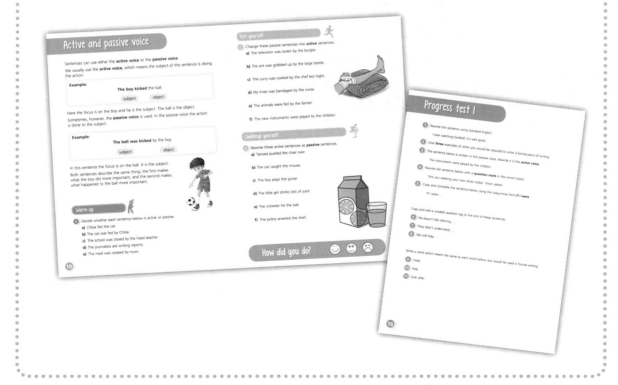

Contents

Formal speech vocabulary   **4**

Personal and impersonal writing   **6**

Double negatives   **8**

Active and passive voice   **10**

Questions and question tags   **12**

Subjunctive forms   **14**

Progress test 1   **16**

Expanded noun phrases   **18**

Adverbials in a paragraph   **20**

Layout   **22**

Determiners and articles   **24**

Synonyms   **26**

Antonyms   **28**

Progress test 2   **30**

Colons and semi-colons   **32**

Brackets and dashes   **34**

Ellipses   **36**

Bullet points   **38**

Hyphens   **40**

Progress test 3   **42**

Answers (centre pull-out)   **1–4**

Formal speech vocabulary

Speech needs to be appropriate for the audience. There is a clear difference between using vocabulary suitable for a conversation with friends and formal vocabulary.

When speaking in formal situations such as interviews, or to unknown people and when giving presentations, formal vocabulary is used. This keeps the meaning the same but demonstrates to the listener or reader that there is an awareness of the importance of the situation and/or audience.

Examples:

Every day speech	Formal Speech
Find out	Discover
Ask for	Request
Go in	Enter

Warm up

1 Copy and match the everyday speech on the left to the corresponding formal speech on the right.

    a) I'm sorry   receive

    b) need   assist

    c) get   I apologise

    d) buy   children

    e) help   require

    f) make better   improve

    g) kids   purchase

2 Copy and complete each sentence to show you understand the meaning of the formal speech.

    a) I require…

    b) I recently purchased…

    c) You will receive…

    d) He apologised…

3 Think of formal vocabulary for the following words or phrases.

a) start

b) end

c) seen

d) stop

e) fix

f) clever

g) get ready

h) write back

Challenge yourself

4 Here is a letter written using everyday / informal speech. Rewrite the letter using formal vocabulary so that it can be sent to the manager of a local newspaper.

> To Sir/Madam,
>
> I am writing to let you know that me and my friends are trying to get some money for our school library. Can you put a notice in your paper asking if anyone would like to give our school some money? We'd use the money people have given us to buy new books, CDs and story sacks.
>
> I hope you can help us.
>
> Thanks a lot.
>
> Lacey

Personal and impersonal writing

When we write we need to be sure that the language we use is **appropriate**.

Either standard or non-standard English can be used in **personal writing**, but this type of writing often has a chatty (colloquial) style and generally makes use of contractions, such as **I'm**, **isn't**, etc. Personal writing is used in texts such as blogs, emails, text messages and notes. Here is an example of the personal form:

> Watch out, guys! I've noticed over the past few weeks the restaurant's been charging people way too much.

Impersonal writing, on the other hand, **always** uses standard English. Contractions are not used and the language is often more formal, matter-of-fact and technical. Complex sentences are also common. Impersonal writing is used in texts such as reports, official letters and formal invitations. Here is an example of the impersonal form:

> Please be aware that it has been brought to our attention in recent weeks that the restaurant has been overcharging its customers.

Warm up

1 Copy the table and place the following texts under **personal** or **impersonal**.

a letter from the gas company   **a text message**

an email to a friend   **a job application**   **a note to your mum**

a police report   **a postcard**   **a letter of complaint**

Personal	Impersonal

2 Read the letter below, which is addressed to the local council.

Hi,

Our bin hasn't been emptied. Can you tell me why not? It is overflowing and there is a lot of rubbish on the floor. It is making our garden look a mess. I need you to sort this problem out. Is that ok?

Love,

Mr Burns

Find **two** examples of inappropriate language in the text and explain why they are inappropriate.

Challenge yourself

3 Rewrite the letter to make it impersonal. You can add more detail, vocabulary and punctuation to improve it.

How did you do?

Double negatives

Double negatives are often used in **dialogue**. They should **not** be used in **standard English** as they are grammatically incorrect and can be quite confusing.

A double negative is when two negative words in a sentence cancel each other out.

Example:

He **can't** play with **nobody**.

The sentence above is incorrect. When written correctly in standard English, the sentence should be:

He **can't** play with **anyone / anybody**.

or

He **can** play with **no one**.

Warm up

1 Which of these sentences are grammatically correct?

   a) I don't listen to anyone.

   b) You're not going nowhere.

   c) The baby can't hardly talk yet.

   d) Don't get into any trouble.

   e) You're not going anywhere.

   f) The baby can hardly talk yet.

   g) Don't get into no trouble.

   h) I don't listen to no one.

2 Choose the correct word to make each sentence grammatically correct.

a) He couldn't find his keys **anywhere / nowhere**.

b) Jessica couldn't find **none / any** of her missing jewellery.

c) I don't need **no one / anyone** to help me with my revision.

d) I did not meet **nobody / anybody** at the disco.

e) My teacher doesn't know **nothing / anything** about the argument in the playground.

f) I didn't do **anything / nothing** wrong.

Challenge yourself

3 Which words fit gaps (a)–(f)?

never	anywhere	any	ever	any	anyone

Dear Sir/Madam,

I am writing to complain about my recent visit to your hotel. When we first saw our room, we were very disappointed. We could not find (a) _____ to put our cases. The beds were small and did not have (b) _____ sheets on.

In the bathroom, the shower was not working very well and the bath was the dirtiest I have (c) _____ seen. Our towels looked dirty too, so we did not want to use them.

When I tried to speak to a member of your staff, I could not find (d) _____ to help me. I have (e) _____ had (f) _____ problems like this before and I sincerely hope that you will refund our money.

Yours faithfully,

Mrs Sams

How did you do?

Active and passive voice

Sentences can use either the **active voice** or the **passive voice**.

We usually use the **active voice**, which means the subject of the sentence is doing the action.

Example:

The boy kicked the ball.

subject   object

Here the focus is on the boy and he is the subject. The ball is the object.

Sometimes, however, the **passive voice** is used. In the passive voice the action is done to the subject.

Example:

The ball was kicked by the boy.

subject   object

In this sentence the focus is on the ball. It is the subject.

Both sentences describe the same thing; the first makes what the boy did more important, and the second makes what happened to the ball more important.

Warm up

1 Decide whether each sentence below is active or passive.

   a) Chloe fed the cat.

   b) The cat was fed by Chloe.

   c) The school was closed by the head teacher.

   d) The journalists are writing reports.

   e) The meal was cooked by mum.

2 Change these passive sentences into **active** sentences.

a) The television was stolen by the burglar.

b) The ant was gobbled up by the large beetle.

c) The curry was cooked by the chef last night.

d) My knee was bandaged by the nurse.

e) The animals were fed by the farmer.

f) The new instruments were played by the children.

Challenge yourself

3 Rewrite these active sentences as **passive** sentences.

a) Tamara pushed the chair over.

b) The cat caught the mouse.

c) The boy plays the guitar.

d) The little girl drinks lots of juice.

e) The cricketer hit the ball.

f) The police arrested the thief.

How did you do?

Questions and question tags

Question marks are needed at the end of **questions** and **question tags**.

A **question tag** is a question added to a statement, exclamation or command that invites the person listening or reading to agree. Question tags are often used in informal English.

Examples:

It's a nice day today, **isn't it**?   Turn it down, **will you**?

Warm up

1. Copy the sentences and then put question marks and full stops in the correct places.

   a) Please can you help me with my homework It is quite difficult

   b) How many weeks are there in a year

   c) Did you prefer watching the film or reading the book I preferred the book

   d) When is it going to stop raining

   e) Do you know when the library is open I need to return some books

   f) Although I am feeling confident now, how do you think I'll feel before the test tomorrow

   g) Can you help me understand this report please

   h) How old was William Shakespeare when he died

2 Identify the question tags in these sentences.

   a) I don't really understand, do you?

   b) You did give your teacher the letter, didn't you?

   c) She has got the correct change, hasn't she?

   d) You were expecting me to arrive today, weren't you?

3 Write a question tag to end the following sentences.

   a) The match this morning was cancelled, …

   b) The doctor's surgery is very busy today, …

   c) The sunshine today is lovely, …

   d) I think he'd like to go to the fun fair tomorrow, …

   e) The new baby is very cute, …

   f) They say exercise is good for everyone, …

Challenge yourself

4 Copy the table below and write a question for each answer (an example has been done for you). Remember to begin the question with a capital letter.

Question	Answer
How many cakes did you eat?	I ate four.
	At the post office.
	No, I'm French.
	Yes, you have!

How did you do?

Subjunctive forms

Sometimes in formal speech or writing the subjunctive is used to indicate that something is doubtful or conditional.

Examples:

If I were rich, then I would buy a new car.

Were they to come and stay, I would be most delighted.

Warm up

1 Write an ending for each of the sentences below that start with the subjunctive.

a) If I were intelligent, …

b) Were she to pass the examination, …

c) If it were not for the dog, …

d) Were I not so afraid, …

e) If they were not so noisy, …

f) Were they to play nearby, …

2 Copy the sentences and complete them with the first part of each subjunctive.

a) If _____ to attend, it would be a fabulous party.

b) _____ to fail, it would be a disappointment.

c) If _____ organized, we would be ready.

d) _____ to marry later, the rain might have stopped.

e) If _____ not for him, we would never have met.

f) If _____ for the wonderful doctors, I may still be in hospital.

Challenge yourself

3 Read the letter of complaint below where a holidaymaker has written to the owner of a campsite.

Rewrite the underlined sentences using the subjunctive form.

Dear Sir/Madam,

I am writing to inform you that we had a very unpleasant stay on your campsite last weekend. Firstly, there was far too much noise. Then we found out that the toilet block was dirty and the facilities were not as clean as we would have liked. <u>We nearly packed our bags and left but it was too late.</u>

The food in your café was very overpriced and it took a long time for the staff to make our sandwiches. <u>We should have made our own but we had no bread!</u>

<u>We would be grateful if you reply to our letter.</u>

Yours faithfully

Mr and Mrs Smithson

How did you do?

Progress test 1

1 Rewrite this sentence using standard English.

I love watching football; it's well good.

2 Give **three** examples of when you would be required to write a formal piece of writing.

3 The sentence below is written in the passive voice. Rewrite it in the **active voice**.

The instruments were played by the children.

4 Rewrite the sentence below with a **question mark** in the correct place.

"Are you wearing your new shoes today" Mum asked.

5 Copy and complete the sentence below using the subjunctive form **If I were**.

If I were…

Copy and add a suitable question tag to the end of these sentences.

6 He doesn't like dancing, …

7 They didn't understand, …

8 We will help, …

Write a word which means the same as each word below, but would be used in formal writing.

9 mate

10 help

11 look after

Rewrite the sentences below to ensure there are no double negatives.

12 The children did not do nothing to upset the neighbours!

13 The school had not got no one away ill.

14–**16** Copy and complete the table below.

Active	Passive
The dog ate Dad's dinner.	
	This tennis racket was designed by top scientists.
	The report was written by the teacher.

17 Write a sentence beginning with the formal subjunctive **Were he to offer**…

18 Identify the question tag in the sentence below.

You can't drive a car, can you?

19 Write a suitable question tag for the sentences below.

We are nearly there, …

20 Write a sentence in the passive voice.

Expanded noun phrases

Detail can be added to a sentence by **expanding** a noun phrase.

One way of doing this is by **adding adjectives**.

> **Example:**
>
> Paul kicked the ball. ⟶ Paul kicked the **bouncy**, **blue** ball.

Another way is by **adding a prepositional phrase**.

> **Example:**
>
> Paul kicked the bouncy, ⟶ Paul kicked the bouncy, blue ball
> blue ball. **with yellow stripes**.

You can also use a **relative clause**.

> **Example:**
>
> Paul kicked the bouncy, ⟶ Paul kicked the bouncy, blue ball
> blue ball in the park. with yellow stripes **that my dad bought me for my birthday**.

In this way a noun phrase can be built up in stages.

> **Example:**
>
> The dog.
> The clever dog.
> The clever old dog.
> The clever old dog with a stick.
> The clever old dog with a stick in the park.
> The clever old dog with a stick in the park that is waiting patiently.

1 Expand the noun phrases in the sentences below.
Use an adjective, a prepositional phrase and a relative clause at least once.

   a) the television

   b) those boys

   c) your dress

   d) his cat

   e) their bed

   f) my cousin

2 Add an expanded noun phrase to complete these sentences.

   a) Michael ran up the hill towards...

   b) We enjoy playing outside in the...

   c) I am having a sleepover at...

   d) Martha waited for...

   e) The news reporter recorded the...

   f) We walked along the beach towards...

3 Write a paragraph about yourself using expanded noun phrases.

How did you do?

Adverbials in a paragraph

In non-fiction writing, ideas are grouped into paragraphs to make the facts clear to the reader and to organize the writing.

In a recount, explanation text, information text, persuasion text and discussion text, adverbials are often used within a paragraph.

Example:

Some people believe that mice are useful, entertaining animals. *On the other hand*, some think they are a nuisance and would not make a suitable pet.

Adverbials can also come at the beginning of a paragraph.
They can link paragraphs together.

Example:

Rats are too big to be a domestic pet.

In contrast, a mouse or hamster are small animals and need very little space.

Warm up

1 Read the sentences below and copy out the adverbial in each sentence.

   a) The USA is a large country compared with England.

   b) As a consequence, the sea is very rough during the winter months.

   c) Unfortunately, the road was blocked.

   d) Despite these things, there is clear progress.

   e) Children in Year 6 prefer going to the cinema, whereas the children in Year 5 prefer watching a film at home.

   f) It could be argued that schools should open at weekends.

   g) Equally, other children think they should be allowed to own a mobile phone.

2 Choose a suitable adverbial from below for the start of each sentence **a)–f)**.

As a consequence   **On the other hand**   **Finally**

      Alternatively   **Unfortunately**   **It is clear that**

a) _____, I think that children should wear school uniform.

b) _____, the teachers said no.

c) _____, to conclude our ideas we need to answer the original question.

d) _____, some people argue zoos should be banned and closed in our country.

e) _____, children are doing less exercise.

f) _____, the World Cup was a success.

3 For each topic below write a paragraph of your own using adverbials.

a) Should PE be taught in schools every day?

b) Public transport should be cheaper for everyone.

c) Head teachers should give pupils extra holidays.

How did you do?

Layout

The layout of writing (usually non-fiction) can be organized in a variety of ways depending on its purpose.

Writing can be presented in a range of layouts including:

- Bullet points
- Numbered bullet points
- Tables
- Captions
- Columns

Headings and subheadings can be used to let readers know what a paragraph is about. They make the writing clear and structured.

Subheadings allow the writer to organize sentences into categories or 'points' within a paragraph.

Headings and subheadings can be a statement, exclamation or a question.

Writing can be presented in many different forms. Sometimes lists or 'spider' diagrams can be used to plan ideas or present information.

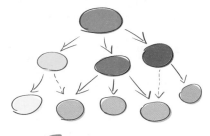

Warm up

1. Copy and match each type of writing on the left to one of the layout features that it might include on the right.

Newspaper report	table
Comparison chart	numbered bullet points
Recipe to bake a cake	columns
A debate on eating meat	bullet points
A shopping list	subheadings

Answers

Pages 4–5

1.
   a) I'm sorry = I apologise
   b) need = require
   c) get = receive
   d) buy = purchase
   e) help = assist
   f) make better = improve
   g) kids = children

2. **Accept any suitable answer that makes sense and is grammatically correct.**

3. **Accept any suitable vocabulary. For example:**
   a) begin, commence
   b) finish, conclude
   c) noticed, viewed
   d) halt, terminate
   e) mend, adjust, repair
   f) intelligent, knowledgeable, bright
   g) prepare, arrange
   h) reply, respond

4. **Example only – other words used are correct if meaning is unchanged.**

Dear Sir /Madam

I am writing to **inform you** that **my friends and I are attempting to raise** some money for our school library. **Would it be possible to display** a notice in your paper **requesting whether** anyone would like to **donate money to** our school. **We would** use the money people have **donated** to **purchase** new books, CDs and story sacks.
I hope you can **assist** us.

Yours faithfully

Lacey Smith

Pages 6–7

1.

Personal	Impersonal
a text message	a letter from the gas company
an email to a friend	a job application
a note to your mum	a police report
a postcard	a letter of complaint

2. **Accept any of the following: The use of 'Hi' is too informal / personal; The use of 'hasn't' is too informal / personal; 'Is that ok?' is too informal / personal; 'Love, Mr Burns' is too informal / personal; There are no complex sentences. / The sentences are all very short.**

3. **The letter should have correct grammar and punctuation, an impersonal greeting (e.g. Dear Sir / Madam) and sign-off (e.g. Yours faithfully), complex sentences, and formal, matter-of-fact vocabulary.**

Pages 8–9

1.
   a) I don't listen to anyone. ✓
   b) You're not going nowhere. ✗
   c) The baby can't hardly talk yet. ✗
   d) Don't get into any trouble. ✓
   e) You're not going anywhere. ✓
   f) The baby can hardly talk yet. ✓
   g) Don't get into no trouble. ✗
   h) I don't listen to no one. ✗

2.
   a) anywhere   b) any
   c) anyone   d) anybody
   e) anything   f) anything

3.
   a) anywhere   b) any
   c) ever   d) anyone
   e) never   f) any

Pages 10–11

1.
   a) active   b) passive
   c) passive   d) active
   e) passive

2.
   a) The burglar stole the television.
   b) The large beetle gobbled up the ant.
   c) The chef cooked the curry last night.
   d) The nurse bandaged my knee.
   e) The farmer fed the animals.
   f) The children played the new instruments.

3.
   a) The chair was pushed over by Tamara.
   b) The mouse was caught by the cat.
   c) The guitar is played by the boy.
   d) Lots of juice is drunk by the little girl.
   e) The ball was hit by the cricketer.
   f) The thief was arrested by the police.

Pages 12–13

1.
   a) Please can you help me with my homework? It is quite difficult.
   b) How many weeks are there in a year?
   c) Did you prefer watching the film or reading the book? I preferred the book.
   d) When is it going to stop raining?
   e) Do you know when the library is open? I need to return some books.
   f) Although I am feeling confident now, how do you think I'll feel before the test tomorrow?
   g) Can you help me understand this report please?
   h) How old was William Shakespeare when he died?

2.
   a) I don't really understand, <u>do you</u>?
   b) You did give your teacher the letter, <u>didn't you</u>?
   c) She has got the correct change, <u>hasn't she</u>?
   d) You were expecting me to arrive today, <u>weren't you</u>?

3. **Accept any suitable, grammatically correct question tags. For example:**
   a) wasn't it?
   b) isn't it
   c) isn't it?
   d) wouldn't he?
   e) isn't it/he/she?
   f) don't they?

4. **Accept any suitable, grammatically correct questions. For example:** Where did you buy stamps? Are you English? Have I got it right?

Pages 14–15

1. **Accept any suitable ending. For example:**
   a) I would pass all the exams.
   b) her parents would be very proud.
   c) I would not be at the park.
   d) I would walk to school on my own.
   e) I would not have a headache.
   f) I would be allowed to go.

2. **Accept any correct subjunctive using any correct pronoun. For example:**
   a) I were
   b) Were they/was I/were he/were she
   c) we were
   d) Were we
   e) it were
   f) it were not

3. Example answer:

Dear Sir / Madam,

I am writing to inform you that we had a very unpleasant stay on your campsite last weekend. Firstly, there was far too much noise. Then we found out that the toilet block was dirty and the facilities were not as clean as we would have liked. Were it not so late, we would have left. The food in your café was very overpriced and it took a long time for the staff to make our sandwiches. Were we to have had any bread, we would have made our own!

If you were to respond to our letter, then we would be most grateful.

Yours faithfully

Mr and Mrs Smithson

Pages 16–17
1. I love watching football; it is very good.
2. **Any suitable examples, e.g.** letter of complaint, formal invitation, report to a school
3. The children played the instruments.
4. "Are you wearing your new shoes today?" Mum asked.
5. **Any suitable ending**
   e.g. naughty, I would break the glass on purpose.
6. does he?
7. did they?
8. won't we?
9.–11. **Any suitable word, e.g.**
   friend/companion
   assist/aid
   care for/comfort
12. The children did nothing to upset the neighbours **or** The children did not do anything to upset the neighbours.
13. The school hadn't got anyone away ill.
14–16.

Active	Passive
The dog ate Dad's dinner.	Dad's dinner was eaten by the dog.
Top scientists designed the tennis racket.	The tennis racket was designed by top scientists.
The teacher wrote the report.	The report was written by the teacher.

17. **Any suitable sentence e.g.** were he to offer me some money, I would refuse it.
18. You can't drive a car, can you?
19. **Any suitable question tag e.g.** aren't we?
20. **Any suitable sentence written in the passive voice correctly.**

Pages 18–19
1. a)–f) **Accept any suitable expanded noun phrases. For example:**
   a) Alex watched the blaring TV that was perched on the shelf in the lounge.
2. a)–f) **Accept any suitable expanded noun phrase to complete each sentence. For example:**
   a) Michael ran up the hill towards his waving friends.
3. **Accept any suitable answer using expanded noun phrases.**

Pages 20–21
1. a) compared with
   b) As a consequence
   c) Unfortunately
   d) Despite
   e) whereas
   f) It could be argued that
   g) Equally

2. **The most suitable answers are:**
   a) On the other hand
   b) Unfortunately
   c) Finally
   d) Alternatively
   e) As a consequence
   f) It is clear that
3. a), b), c)
   Accept any suitable paragraph which uses adverbials and is about the topic given.

Pages 22–23
1. Newspaper report = columns
   Comparison chart = table
   Recipe to bake a cake = numbered bullet points
   A debate on meat eating = subheadings
   A shopping list = bullet points
2. **Any suitable subheading**

Heading	Subheading
Lion escaped	Recent sightings
Midlands town flooded	Location
The cost of mobile phones	Price increases
Evacuation in the second world war	Where did the children go?
Life in space	What did the astronauts eat and drink?
A new supermarket opening	Opening times

3. **Accept any suitable layout using subheadings and the correct information for each subheading underneath. For example: Maths / English / Science / Targets**

Pages 24–25
1. a) The/a
   b) a
   c) an
2. **Accept any suitable word.**
3. a) a clarinet
   b) an egg
   c) a coat
   d) a computer
   e) a book
   f) an injury
4. a) I need to wear a jumper and a coat.
   b) I saw an ant crawling along the floor
   c) When I go to the shops, I need to buy a magazine.
   d) The babysitter read a / the story before the children went to bed.
   e) Jamie had a broken ankle after falling down the stairs.
5. a) Aalam likes watching the TV in the morning before going to school.
   b) An animal from the rescue centre needs rehoming.
   c) Ana listens to the radio for an hour while she is getting ready to go out.
   d) A little girl in the nursery had a tummy ache and wanted a drink of water.
   e) An aeroplane landed at an airport at exactly 10.05.
   f) The playground will be closed on Monday and Tuesday because the council are repairing the equipment.
   g) Emma wants to adopt an elephant at the local wildlife park.
   h) The children played on an indoor trampoline for over an hour.

Pages 26–27

1. **Any suitable synonyms, e.g.**
   tiny, minute, little
   wealthy,
   poorly, sick
   fragile, delicate
   quick, speedy,
   show
   cheerful
2. **Accept any suitable answers that use synonyms correctly.**
3. a) brave
   b) angry
   c) quiet
   d) insignificant
   e) rough
   f) naughty
4. **Possible answers:**
   a) shouted
   b) cheerful
   c) angry
   d) anxious
   e) apologetic
   f) colourful
5. **Examples only:**
   a) upset – I was upset because I had no one to play with.
   b) show – I wanted to perform in our class show.
   c) mumble – My dad will mumble so I struggle to hear him.
   d) bake – I like to bake cakes.
   e) even – I keep an even hand when sewing.
   f) dead – the flowers look dead.
   g) serenade – I will serenade my family
   h) vanish – My sister will vanish when we have to tidy up.

Pages 28–29

1. **Accept any suitable antonym. For example:**
   a) large
   b) poor
   c) healthy
   d) strong
   e) slow
   f) conceal, hide
   g) sad, unhappy
2. **Accept any suitable answers using antonyms correctly.**
3. a) fake
   b) pull
   c) late
   d) exterior / outside
   e) exhale
   f) empty
4. **Accept any suitable antonym used correctly in a sentence. For example:**
   a) short – The little man was very short.
   b) worst – The worst thing about being ill is not seeing your friends.
   c) depart – the train will depart at 15.00
   d) full – I am feeling very full
   e) float – the toys will float in the bath.
   f) unforgiving – The class were unforgiving to the teacher.
   g) clever – the clever girl read lots of books.
   h) calm – I felt calm before the exams

Pages 30–31

1. **Accept any three. For example:** table, subheading, heading, bullet points, numbered bullet points, title, caption, label, columns.
2. an engine
3. a train
4. The old dog barked at the young child.
5. **Possible answers:** When comparing things, to present information clearly using more than one viewpoint.

Accept any suitable expanded noun phrase. For example:

6. The lion roared at the wildlife park this morning.
7. I baked a cake in the kitchen.
8. **Possible answer:** Tomorrow, we will be looking for a new house and searching for a new school.
9. nice/gentle
10. report (news report)
11. **Accept any suitable sentence, e.g.** On the other hand, it is very clear to see that all children should eat a school dinner.
12. baby
13. noisy
14–16. Examples only

Word	Synonym	Antonym
clean	hygienic tidy neat	dirty smelly
guilty	wrong blameworthy	guiltless right innocent
noisy	loud	quiet

17. an angel
18. a helicopter
19. a pig
20. To organize the writing, to tell the reader what the next paragraph will be about, to help the reader find what they are looking for quickly.

Pages 32–33

1. a) There are seven colours in the rainbow: red, orange, yellow, green, blue, indigo and violet.
   b) Samantha burnt her hand on the kettle: she touched it when it had just boiled.
2. Dogs make good pets: they are loyal to their owners.
   Sophie liked watching sport; football was her favourite.
   We go to school five days a week: Monday, Tuesday, Wednesday, Thursday and Friday.
   The ice cream shop was fantastic; the other shops weren't bad.
3. **Accept any grammatically correct clauses that are related to the openers without explaining them.**
   For example:
   a) I went to France on holiday; you went to Greece.

Pages 34–35

1. **Correct answers:**
   a) Spain (a country in Europe) is a popular holiday destination for British tourists.
   d) For dinner, I ate sandwiches (and crisps).
2. a) The River Trent (in Nottinghamshire) is a long river.
   b) Tap dancing (although it is hard to do) is lots of fun.
   c) Luke's dad is good at playing darts (or so he thinks!)
   d) June (half way through the year) is a summer month.
   e) An English breakfast (bacon, eggs, beans, and sausages) is a good way to start the day!
3. a) The River Trent -in Nottinghamshire- is a long river.
   b) Tap dancing -although it is hard to do- is lots of fun.
   c) Luke's dad is good at playing darts -or so he thinks!
   d) June -half way through the year- is a summer month.
   e) An English breakfast -bacon, eggs, beans, and sausages- is a good way to start the day!
4. (In a helpless voice)
   (Picking up the first bowl and licking the spoon)
   (Picking up the second bowl, sniffing the porridge and then licking the spoon)

Pages 36–37

1. a) faltering train of thought
   b) pauses
   c) dramatic silence

2.
   a) Just then... the bell rang. / Just then the bell rang...
   b) It was red... shiny... amazing!
   c) "You could... you know... not bother," he said.

3.
   a) Jane Austen said, "We have all a better guide in ourselves... than any other person can be."
   b) Charles Dickens said, "There is nothing so strong... as the simple truth."
   c) Marcus Aurelius said, "Look back over the past... and you can foresee the future, too."

Pages 38–39

1.
   a) numbered
   b) numbered
   c) plain
   d) plain

2.
   a)
     1. To make a cup of tea, first fill the kettle with cold water.
     2. Then turn the kettle on and wait for it to boil.
     3. Put a teabag into a cup and carefully pour the boiling water into the cup.
     4. Then take the tea bag out and add some milk or sugar.
   b) Please come to our school fair. There will be lots of great stalls where you can buy things and have a go playing some games.
     There will be:
     • a raffle
     • a tombola
     • a toy stall
     • book stall
     • cake sale too
   c) For the school residential trip next week everyone will need to bring:
     • some warm clothes
     • a washbag
     • a torch
     • a blanket
     • a pillow
     • a blanket
   d) The agenda for our meeting will include four main items:
     1. Welcome new members.
     2. Discuss school homework.
     3. Talk about sports day.
     4. Suggest ways to keep our school cleaner.

3. Any suitable ideas
   a) Caring for a dog = plain bullets
   b) How to build a model out of bricks = numbered bullets

Pages 40–41

1.
   a) a small-business man
   b) re-cover your books
   c) recover your books
   d) A small business man

2.
spider–eating bird = a bird that eats spiders
spider eating bird = a spider eating a bird.
take-away food = food bought at a fast food restaurant
take away food = take his food away from him.
Three-week holidays for sale = There are holidays lasting three weeks for sale.
Three week holidays for sale = There are 3 holidays for sale, each lasting a week.

3.
   a) A crocodile that eats humans.
   b) A man eating a crocodile.
   c) 4 one year olds.
   d) All children who are four.
   e) A car is chasing a dog.
   f) The dog chases cars.
   g) Water for humans to drink.
   h) Human having a drink of water.

4. Accept any suitable words or phrases.

Pages 42–43

1. Accept any suitable sentence. For example:
I jumped… I jumped again...then I stood frozen, silent and still.

2. It's a very confusing map; on the other hand, it might show us the way.

3. Zanda laughed loudly; Freddie giggled.

4. June has 30 days; July has 31.

5. Boys and girls, you need to be quiet; the story is about to start.

6. Any suitable sentence, e.g.
Elise played on the swings: she went very high!

7. James (12) scored the winning goal in the football match (against Ravenschurch Football Club).

8. Mr Stone (the Year 6 teacher) read the class a story (set in America).

9. A fire fighter (from Norfolk) rescued a passenger from a car (near the river).

10. Any of the following:
Pauses, faltering train of thought,
Dramatic silence,
Trailing off mid sentence

11. A balanced diet - that includes fruit and vegetables - helps us to keep healthy.

12. Accept any ingredients as long as bullet points are used, e.g.
   • bread
   • butter
   • filling (e.g. cheese, tomato)

13. Accept any answers as long as there are four clear steps in the process.

14. Any correct sentence, e.g.
Cardiff (the capital city of Wales) is home to the Millennium stadium.

15. When using chronological order i.e. instructions.

16. a) child-like monkey

17. Any suitable sentence, e.g. I like playing the following games: skipping, dodge ball and hide and seek.

18. a) Ellipses

19. a colon

20. Any suitable answer, e.g.
My favourite colours are: red, blue, yellow and green.

2 Copy and complete the table. Write a suitable subheading that may be used to match each heading. An example has been done for you.

Heading	Subheading
Lion escaped	Recent sightings
Midlands town flooded	
The cost of mobile phones	
Evacuation in the second world war	
Life in space	
A new supermarket opening	

Challenge yourself

3 Look at the school report for a Year 6 pupil below. Organise the text using **layout features** to make the report structured and clear.

Daisy's school report

In Maths, Daisy can use her understanding of place value to multiply and divide whole numbers and decimals. She knows all of her multiplication facts including the 7, 8, 9, 10, 11 and 12 times tables. Daisy needs to practise solving sums involving fractions and decimals as she often gets muddled with these.

Daisy is a very fluent reader and enjoys reading a range of fiction and non-fiction. She especially likes reading and performing aloud to the class. Daisy needs to work harder with her writing, especially when organizing her ideas using layout features of non-fiction texts.

Daisy enjoys all her science work and has made excellent progress in the following areas: states of matter, sound and electricity. To progress further in this subject she could plan different enquiries to answer questions and use test results to make further predictions.

How did you do?

Determiners and articles

A **determiner** stands before a noun or a word that describes the noun (an adjective). The most common determiners are **the**, **a** and **an**. These are also known as **articles**.

Before a word beginning with a consonant sound we use **a**, but before a word beginning with a vowel sound we use **an** (sometimes **h** at the start of a word can be silent, so we use **an** rather than **a**).

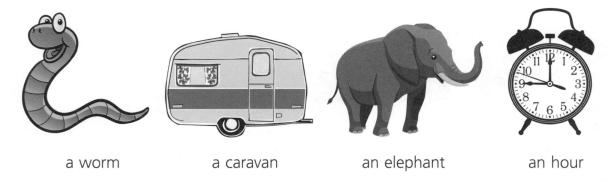

| a worm | a caravan | an elephant | an hour |

Warm up

1 Identify the determiners in each sentence below.

    a) The girl put on a cardigan.

    b) I need a drink.

    c) I don't want to be an actor in the game.

2 Copy and fill the table below with words that would follow a or *an*. Two examples have been done for you.

a	an
fireman	apple

3 Read the words and decide whether to use *a* or *an*

a) clarinet

b) egg

c) coat

d) computer

e) book

f) injury

Challenge yourself

4 Choose *a*, *an* or *the* to complete the sentences.

a) I need to wear _____ jumper and _____ coat.

b) I saw _____ ant crawling along _____ floor.

c) When I go to _____ shops, I need to buy _____ magazine.

d) _____ babysitter read _____ story before _____ children went to bed.

e) Jamie had _____ broken ankle after falling down _____ stairs.

5 Rewrite these sentences correctly, replacing *a*, *an* or *the* with the correct determiner.

a) Aalam likes watching TV in an morning before going to school.

b) A animal from the rescue centre needs rehoming.

c) Ana listens to an radio for a hour while she is getting ready to go out.

d) An little girl in the nursery had the tummy ache and wanted an drink of water.

e) A aeroplane landed at a airport at exactly 10.05.

f) A playground will be closed on Monday and Tuesday because a council are repairing an equipment.

g) Emma wants to adopt a elephant at an local wildlife park.

h) The children played on a indoor trampoline for over the hour.

How did you do?

Synonyms

Synonyms are words that have the same or similar meaning.

Examples:

clever = intelligent

big = large

old = ancient

Using a variety of synonyms in speech and writing makes it more interesting to the listener and reader.

Synonyms can be found by using a **thesaurus**.

Warm up

1 Copy and complete the table below by adding one or more synonyms for each word.

Word	Synonyms
small	
rich	
ill	
weak	
fast	
reveal	
happy	

2 Write sentences for **three** of the synonyms from the table in question 1.

3 Find the odd word out in each list of synonyms.

  a) careful, cautious, brave

  b) rude, bad–mannered, cheeky, angry

  c) miserable, quiet, gloomy, sad,

  d) insignificant, amazing, unbelievable, fabulous

  e) gentle, soft, rough, tender

  f) sleepy, naughty, tired, drowsy

Challenge yourself

4 Write a synonym for each word below.

  a) declared

  b) happy

  c) cross

  d) worried

  e) sorry

  f) bright

5 Write a synonym for each word below and then write it in a sentence.

  a) tearful

  b) play

  c) whisper

  d) cook

  e) steady

  f) lifeless

  g) sing

  h) disappear

How did you do?

Antonyms

Antonyms are words that have the **opposite** meaning.

> **Example:**
>
> clever = stupid
>
> big = small
>
> old = new

Antonyms are the opposite of synonyms.

Warm up

1) Copy and complete the table below by adding one or more antonyms for each word.

Word	Antonyms
small	
rich	
ill	
weak	
fast	
reveal	
happy	

2) Write sentences for **three** of your antonyms from the table in question 1.

3 What is the missing antonym for each of these sentences?

a) The *real* celebrity was not impressed with the _____ impersonator.

b) *Push* the door to open it and _____ it to close.

c) I like to be *early* for school but my sister is always _____.

d) The *interior* of our school is extremely neat and tidy but the _____ is a mess.

e) When you breathe in you *inhale* and when you breathe out you _____.

f) There is an _____ room next door. This one is fully *occupied*.

Challenge yourself

4 Write an antonym for each word below and then write it in a sentence.

a) tall

b) best

c) arrive

d) empty

e) sink

f) forgiving

g) foolish

h) worried

How did you do?

Progress test 2

1 Write three different layout devices.

Write either a or an before each noun

2 _____ engine

3 _____ train

4 Copy the sentence below and underline the pair of antonyms.

The old dog barked at the young child.

5 Give an example of when you might use a table in a piece of writing.

Expand the noun phrases in the sentences below.

6 The lion roared.

7 I baked a cake.

8 Choose a pair of synonyms to complete the sentence below.

Tomorrow, we will be _____ for a new house and _____ for a new school.

9 Replace the word **'kind'** in the sentence below with a suitable synonym.

"Remember to be kind to each other," the parents told their children as they went outside to play.

10 Give an example of a type of text you might see written in columns.

11 Write a sentence starting with 'On the other hand…'

Look at the sentence below. The noun phrase has been underlined.

The noisy baby cried all night.

12 Which word in the noun phrase is the noun?

13 Which word in the noun phrase is the adjective?

14 – 16 Copy and complete the table.

For each given word insert a synonym and an antonym.

Word	Synonym	Antonym
clean		
guilty		
noisy		

Add the correct determiner to the words below.

17 _____ angel

18 _____ helicopter

19 _____ pig.

20 Explain why a heading or a subheading is used in non-fiction writing.

Colons and semi-colons

A **colon** can be used to introduce lists, quotations or examples.

> **Example:**
>
> I like eating the following vegetables: carrots, cauliflower, broccoli and potatoes.

A colon can be used to join two main clauses (or even two sentences) if the second one **explains** the first.

> **Examples:**
>
> Matthew ran along the beach: he was full of energy.

A **semi-colon** indicates a longer pause than a comma and is used between two main clauses that are closely linked.

> **Example:**
>
> Matthew ran along the beach; Jessica walked along.

Semi-colons can also be used to separate items in complex lists.

Warm up

1. Which **two** of the following sentences use a **colon** correctly?

   a) There are seven colours in the rainbow: red, orange, yellow, green, blue, indigo and violet.

   b) Samantha burnt her hand on the kettle: she touched it when it had just boiled.

   c) Ruben liked the strawberries: Becky liked the cake.

   d) The sun was shining yesterday: today it is raining.

2 Join the broken sentences with a colon or semi-colon.
Copy and write the completed sentences.

Dogs make good pets	the other shops weren't bad.
Sophie liked watching sport	Monday, Tuesday, Wednesday, Thursday and Friday.
We go to school five days a week	football was her favourite.
The ice cream shop was fantastic	they are loyal to their owners.

Challenge yourself

3 Complete these sentences so that the **semi-colons** are used correctly.
Remember, the second clause should not explain the first; it should just be related.

a) I went to France on holiday; …

b) The teacher laughed; …

c) Maisie read a book; …

d) Water keeps us healthy; …

How did you do?

Brackets and dashes

Brackets, dashes and commas can be used to insert a parenthesis into a sentence. A parenthesis is usually a word, phrase or clause that gives additional information and makes a sentence more detailed.

> **Example:**
>
> Michael Tombs (age 69) was rushed to hospital.

Brackets can be used to allow the writer to speak directly to the reader in an aside comment.

> **Example:**
>
> As the driver stopped the car (a little too sudden for my liking) I spotted a lion in the bushes.

Brackets can also be used when giving stage directions in play scripts.

> **Example:**
>
> King: (placing his crown on the table) Whoever finds my daughter will receive a reward.

Brackets are often called parentheses.

Sometimes dashes can be used instead of parentheses if the extra information needs more emphasis or if the writer is creating tension.

1 Which **two** sentences use parentheses correctly?

a) Spain (a country in Europe) is a popular holiday destination for British tourists.

b) The film at the cinema (starts at 6.30 p.m.)

c) (Swimming) is a good form of exercise for everybody.

d) For dinner, I ate sandwiches (and crisps).

Test yourself

2 Copy these sentences and add brackets.

a) The River Trent in Nottinghamshire is a long river.

b) Tap dancing although it is hard to do is lots of fun.

c) Luke's dad is good at playing darts or so he thinks!

d) June half way through the year is a summer month.

e) A traditional English breakfast bacon, eggs, beans, and sausages is a good way to start the day!

Challenge yourself

3 Rewrite three of the sentences from question 2 using **dashes** instead of brackets.

4 Copy the play script below. Add parentheses in the correct places to show stage directions.

Goldilocks: In a helpless voice. I'm hungry. I wonder what the bears are having for breakfast?

Narrator: Goldilocks entered the three bears house cautiously then ran straight into the kitchen.

Goldilocks: Picking up the first bowl and licking the spoon. This porridge is too hot.

Goldilocks: Picking up the second bowl, sniffing the porridge and then licking the spoon. This porridge is too cold.

Goldilocks: Tasting the final bowl of porridge. This porridge is just right. I will eat it all up.

How did you do?

Ellipses

An **ellipsis** is a row of three dots.

It is an important cohesive device and can be used to show a pause, a faltering train of thought, a dramatic silence, or when someone has trailed off mid-sentence.

Examples:

Pauses:
Something moved**...** something small**...** something furry!

Faltering train of thought:
Well… we could do it… I suppose.

Dramatic silence:
Just then he stopped…

Trailing off mid-sentence:
I like it, but…

In **formal writing**, an ellipsis is often used to show where words have been left out of a quotation in order to make it shorter.

Example:

If a teacher says,
"All schools, where parents trust that their children will be protected, **should be safe,"** you could use an ellipsis and quote the teacher as saying,
"All schools ... should be safe."

Warm up

1 Read the sentences below. For each sentence, decide whether the ellipsis/ellipses are used to show **pauses**, a **faltering train of thought** or a **dramatic silence**.

a) "Nobody will notice if…" thought Sam.

b) On your marks… get set… go!

c) The door creaked open… the floorboards squeaked.

2 Rewrite these sentences putting ellipsis/ellipses in a suitable place.

a) Just then the bell rang.

b) It was red shiny amazing!

c) "You could you know not bother," he said.

Challenge yourself

3 Read the statements below written by famous authors. For each author, write a sentence using an ellipsis that only quotes their **words in bold**.

Example:

> **Some are born great**, some achieve greatness, **and some have greatness thrust upon them**. (William Shakespeare)

> William Shakespeare said, "**Some are born great ... and some have greatness thrust upon them.**"

a) We have all a better guide in ourselves, if we would attend to it, **than any other person can be**. (Jane Austen)

b) There is nothing so strong or safe in an emergency of life **as the simple truth**. (Charles Dickens)

c) Look back over the past, with its changing empires that rose and fell, **and you can foresee the future, too**. (Marcus Aurelius)

How did you do?

Bullet points

Bullet points are a type of layout feature.

They are used to list information.

Bullet points can either be numbered or left plain.

Numbered bullet points are used when writing is in chronological order.

Examples:

Instructions

1) cut shapes

2) glue shapes together

3) hang using string

Recipe:

1) mix flour and salt

2) add water, yeast and sugar

3) knead the dough with your hands

4) shape and place in a hot oven

Sometimes instead of using numbers, letters can be used. These are often seen in questions on tests or exams.

Plain bullet points are used when information is in written in non-chronological order.

Examples:

Shopping list

- eggs
- butter
- milk

Exercise

- keeps you healthy
- improves your mood
- can be sociable

Each new bullet point starts on a new line.

Warm up

1) Which of the text types below would use numbered bullet points and which would use plain bullet points?

   a) Instructions to build a bookcase

   b) The life cycle of a frog

   c) Facts about the moon

   d) A report of a football match

2 Rewrite these sentences using either numbered or plain bullet points.

a) To make a cup of tea, first fill the kettle with cold water. Then turn the kettle on and wait for it to boil. Put a teabag into a cup and carefully pour the boiling water into the cup. Then take the tea bag out and add some milk or sugar.

b) Please come to our school fair. There will be lots of great stalls where you can buy things and have a go playing some games. There will be a raffle, a tombola, a toy stall, book stall and a cake sale too.

c) For the school residential trip next week everyone will need to bring some warm clothes, a washbag, a torch, a blanket, a pillow and a blanket.

d) The agenda for our meeting will include four main items. First we will welcome new members, then we will discuss school homework, then we will talk about sports day and then we will suggest ways to keep our school cleaner.

3 Write four bullet points for each given subject.
Decide whether to number the bullet points or leave them plain.

a) Caring for a dog

b) How to build a model out of bricks

How did you do?

Hyphens

Hyphens are dashes between two words.

Hyphens are used to clarify information and make phrases clear.

Hyphens can be used to avoid ambiguity.

Example:

Green-fingered is a saying which means a person is good at growing plants.

Green fingered implies a person actually has green fingers.

Warm up

① Which phrase below best explains each of the given sentences?

A small-business man   **A small business man**   **Re-cover your books**

Recover your books

a) A man who has a small business.

b) Put a new cover on your books.

c) Find your books (after losing them).

d) A businessman who is small.

2 Copy and match the phrases on the left to their correct meanings on the right.

Spider–eating bird	Take his food away from him.
Spider eating bird	There are holidays lasting three weeks for sale
Take–away food	A bird that eats spiders.
Take away food	Food bought at a fast food restaurant.
Three-week holidays for sale	There are three holidays for sale, each lasting a week.
Three week holidays for sale	A spider is eating a bird.

Challenge yourself

3 Write a sentence for each phrase to show the correct meaning.

  a) A man-eating crocodile

  b) A man eating crocodile

  c) Four year-old children

  d) Four-year-old children

  e) Car chasing dog

  f) Car-chasing dog

  g) Human drinking–water

  h) Human drinking water

4 Make a list of any other words or phrases you can think of that use a hyphen to avoid ambiguity.

How did you do?

Progress test 3

1. Write a sentence that uses ellipses.

Insert a semi-colon in the most appropriate place in each of the sentences below.

2. Its a very confusing map on the other hand, it might show us the way.

3. Zanda laughed loudly Freddie giggled.

4. June has 30 days July has 31.

5. Insert a comma **and** a semi-colon in the most appropriate places in the sentence below.

   Boys and girls you need to be quiet the story is about to start.

6. Write a sentence that contains a colon.

Copy the sentences and insert two sets of brackets so that they are punctuated correctly.

7. James 12 scored the winning goal in the football match against Ravenschurch Football Club.

8. Mr Stone the Year 6 teacher read the class a story set in America.

9. A fire fighter from Norfolk rescued a passenger from a car near the river.

10. Give two reasons an ellipses may be used.

11 Use dashes to punctuate the sentence below correctly.

A balanced diet that includes fruit and vegetables helps us to keep healthy.

12 Use bullet points to list the ingredients you would need to make a cheese and tomato sandwich.

13 Using bullet points, write four steps to show how you would make the sandwich.

14 Write a sentence that uses parenthesis.

15 Give an example of when bullet points may be numbered.

16 Which phrase means *a monkey is acting like a child?* a) or b)?

a) a child-like monkey

b) a child like monkey

17 Write a sentence that uses a colon.

18 What type of punctuation would be used to show a faltering trail of thought?

a) Ellipses

b) Colon

c) Semi-colon

d) Dashes

19 What type of punctuation could be used when a list is introduced?

20 Write a list of colours using the punctuation from question 19.

Start the sentence with: *My favourite colours are…*

Score ⬤/ 20   43

Published by Keen Kite Books
An imprint of HarperCollins*Publishers* Ltd
The News Building, 1 London Bridge Street,
London, SE1 9GF

ISBN 9780008161415

Text and design © 2015 Keen Kite Books, an
imprint of HarperCollins*Publishers* Ltd

Author: Laura Griffiths